Line and Light

Also by Jeffrey Yang

Poetry

No Home Go Home / Go Home No Home
Hey, Marfa
Vanishing-Line
An Aquarium

Translations

City Gate, Open Up by Bei Dao
Uyghurland, the Farthest Exile by Ahmatjan Osman (with the author)
June Fourth Elegies by Liu Xiaobo
East Slope by Su Shi
Rhythm 226: A Translation of the Qian Jia Shi

Edited Volumes

Meaning a Life: An Autobiography by Mary Oppen (expanded edition)
The Sea Is a Continual Miracle: Sea Poems and Other Writings by Walt Whitman
Time of Grief: Mourning Poems
Birds, Beasts, and Seas: Nature Poems from New Directions
Two Lines: Some Kind of Beautiful Signal (with Natasha Wimmer)

Line and Light

Poems

Jeffrey Yang

Graywolf Press

This publication is made possible, in part, by the voters of Minnesota through a Minnesota State Arts Board Operating Support grant, thanks to a legislative appropriation from the arts and cultural heritage fund. Significant support has also been provided by the McKnight Foundation, the Lannan Foundation, the Amazon Literary Partnership, and other generous contributions from foundations, corporations, and individuals. To these organizations and individuals we offer our heartfelt thanks.

Published by Graywolf Press
212 Third Avenue North, Suite 485
Minneapolis, Minnesota 55401

www.graywolfpress.org

Published in the United States of America
Printed in Canada

ISBN 978-1-64445-086-4 (paperback)
ISBN 978-1-64445-174-8 (ebook)

2 4 6 8 9 7 5 3 1
First Graywolf Printing, 2022

Library of Congress Control Number: 2021945915

Cover design: Jeenee Lee Design

Cover art: Kazumi Tanaka, [Lizards], 2017. Chai Rooiboos tea.

for Pusaka

in memory of the ancestors

Contents

I

Langkasuka 3

II

Line and Light 59
Ceiling and Time 63
Stones and Stars 70

III

No Home Go Home / Go Home No Home 75

IV

"It's early, or it's late" 131
Sea Birth See Day 133
Coral for Kamau 135

V

Ancestors 139

Acknowledgments 147

Thus, no matter how insignificant or contemptible my book may be, I have allowed myself to bring it out into the world, and I ask my fellow citizens to read it several times. At the same time I beg those of you who have the means, to buy several copies and to distribute them to those who are themselves unable to purchase it.

—Nikolai Gogol, tr. by Jesse Zeldin

I

Langkasuka

Not the brave alone, they also praise those who know
how to shape images in wood or compose a song
                                        —Yoruba ballad

0

I never follow the straight path. My path is crooked.
                    —Tengku Alias Taib

1

I open my eyes to forget
I close my eyes to remember

2

How did the shadows sway
behind the light?

Reversal is the movement of the way

3

For the dance, the craft, the puppet
the singer of Inner Winds, the orchestra
in the night forest

      called *bunyi sedap*: delicious sounds
      called *angin*: wind, temperament
      called *pohon budi*: life tree

At the opening
in the middle of the muslin screen
a new spoke
on the turning Wheel

4

I am a guest of the gods behind the shadows

5

Or am I geography? A look? A groove
or notch in the Wood? A wisp

of kemenyan? Rama and Sita?
Gendang gamelan? A spice?

That I am a civilization

as it was thought before, a race,

or a religion? *Adab* rites
in relation to the trees?

Custom of silver or silk?

No written records, no ruins
—People of the Wood—
No nation diadem, no interface

Along the fossilized tracks
through the karstic hills
where what vanishing happened

Facing the forest rhinoceros, the tiger

Sea routes open, bestirring winds

down from the Archipelago of Samui
toward the Crater and Hydra high in the sky

Somewhere between Kelantan and Songkhla
around Saiburi, the two ports of Suvarnabhumi
to *the double gates, towers, and pavilions*

Fields of rice on the alluvial plains

Remnants of levees, earthwork ramparts, outline
        of moats
Some coins: Arabic, Chinese, Sassanid silver
Setback raised bricks
        torus thick, found
linga and nandi

Or am I aromatic woods? A dance? Kuda Kepang? Silat
step? Nadaswaram and thavil? A gong? Am I sanctuary?

        called *awan larat*: wandering cloud spirals
        called *gunungan*: stupa mountain peak
        called *mata hati*: inner eye that guides

the soul, more than ritual or tradition, being
alive to sweat, to difficulty, more than breath

Wayang, shadow and image

play, speech unpeeled
imagination

6

Village of Nothingness
Limitless Wilderness
Bird of Pure Emptiness

Idleness without intention

Flowers and Leaves in the Wood
Bunga and Daun in the Kayu

Kala hidden in the Wood

Punca rahsia source
of seed and learning

Semangat in the Wood
spirit of life, indwelling life-force,
mineral soul

as a lover's drawn to her beloved
as rock's long dream, water's
              sleep, night
bloom of daun bakawali

What vitality binds a universe?

Hayseed in the Wood
Bean Sprout in the Wood

Pucuk paku fernshoot, eye-
lash fiddlehead curl

weeds and buds, creepers and wind-
blown tendrils, claws of aloe
telepuk water plant

Makara in the Wood:
              elephant
        trunk, goat
horns, boar
        tusks, heron
              neck, crocodile
        body, fish
tail animal spirit

Vahana for Varuna and Ganga

on perahu boat and door panel
on window lintel and gate handle
on hilt to lotus leaf wings

Flames in the grain, marks
ingrained through the long art

Nik Rashiddin, master woodcarver:

> *We must think of Langkasuka as the current of a spirit,*
> *a landscape . . . a constant reference, a marker, a presence*
> *. . . a pledge to the ancestors, a promise to nature*

A translation
A nameless name

8

As the forest clears, wonder disappears

9

The forest where you dwell, O Sita, is Ayodhya for me
And Ayodhya without you, O Sita, is darkness for me

10

Words spoken, words written
Words so easy to understand and so easy to put into practice
Yet no one can understand them and no one can put them into practice
Words have their ancestor and affairs have their sovereign
People unused to the way are unwilling to understand them
When a few understand we will surely be honored
And so the poets, in worn rags, conceal a priceless piece of jade within

11

The sutras say, "Looking at trees, they walk"

12

To follow the way of heaven is like stretching a bow:
      Press down the high
      Lift up the low
      Take from excess
      Nourish the deficient
Thus the way of heaven is to take from what is in excess to benefit what is deficient
The way of humankind is otherwise: Take from what is deficient and offer what is in excess
But who can take from one's own excess and offer it to heaven?
Perhaps it is possible through poetry
And so the poets nourish and restore without exacting gratitude
Accomplish their task yet can claim no merit
To the extent they are no better than the ordinary

13

After the thunderstorm, the heat

timeless heat, sun's zero incidence

heat of the tropics, Asia's
Golden Chersonese

bursts into colors
flowers and leaves

of Bukit Nanas, the last
patch of old-growth forest

on the heart of the muddy confluence
Jelutong trail to giant crowfoot trunk

ready to uproot earth, wings beat
against the glass tower, feathers fall

fast past the opening crown

14

A rope bridge crosses the abyss

into the conditioned world, cave-
cool corridors, relief from the heat

dimly lit passages
            crooked like thoughts
unleashed

leased stall to stall, glass
walls, ladders
            transect the air

rise and fall, living
shadows of the day's
living

            Marketplace mecca

laksa steam, noon-
            crowds stream,
hijabsters take a wefie
against the atrium railing

            A sheet of music
forgotten in a dressing room:
Piano Sonata, Opus 1

Refuge from the heat
for how long

            sun, shadow
ten thousand things lost
and found

15

What is the nature of the record

where fire meets ice on the islands
at the end of the continent

ten thousand years of existence
for the Selk'nam and Yaghan

sealed not by the snows but by the Angel
of History overwhelmed by the storm?

The dull roar she heard on the shore
while gathering the fish, sky roar

earth rumble, her family came out of
their huts, rushed to the shore, the growing

roar of the waves, wind, water churning,
the woman shouted, "We must save

ourselves from the storm!" Her family
replied, "Yes, let's leave now, quickly,

out to sea!" But her husband, Kemánta,
couldn't swim and refused to go, saying

he'd climb high up and hide among the rocks,
and after the storm cleared, would return

home. "Come with us!" she protested, "We
can't leave you here alone! That other world

of the water is beautiful, too! Please come!"
She urged him on and on until his family

grabbed his arms and pulled him from a rock,
back down to the shore, where three times

he ran to the sea, then stopped at the edge,
turning back. So they dragged him to the water,

tossed him into the sea, and leaped in after him.
Soon, they transformed into dolphins! Kemánta

sank, but his wife lifted him to the surface. He sank
again, but his brothers-in-law, the Ksámenk,

lifted him again. This went on for a long while
but the family stayed together. And then,

gradually, Kemánta learned how to swim!
The family cheered and swam farther out

into the open. Time passed and they never
returned to land, making their new home

in the sea forever, safe from the storm.

16

Follow the old wheel tracks to the nameless name
and accrue virtue in the circulations of the way

17

Late night teh tarik, day
shade, more teh, sleep

among the kingdom of dripping leaves

in the Wood
the shadows the performance
voice and string and drum

     called *dikir barat*: sung quatrains exchanged
     called *sesuai*: harmonious
     called *nyawa*: soul, breath of life

Winds bring us to the place where
sweet incense turns to jasmine water

     called *berjamu*: feasting, propitiating the spirits
     called *lagu berjalan*: traveling music between states of awareness
     called *sentuhan hati*: heart's intuition

Winds take us away, unsettled,
unquelled, inner gates released

Sun bear and cloud leopard, leatherback
dugong, brother and sister weaver ants,

metallic moths soft, iridescent triangle spots
green wing tip to tip, feathery, crimson neck-

band Birdwing, carrying the beauty of the past
into the present, outlasts the present, nature's gift

Of birds, each bird a soul reflected, reflect-
ing subject dissolution, earth's vanishing blue-

billed gapers trogons *kap-kap* honeysuckers
weavers bee-eaters hornbills *birik-birik*

thrushes flycatcher flames a paradise of birds

Beetles wood-feeders leeches stone field
fissures of ferns phycobiont lichen blossoms

Breathe into tree-frog glide

       through spirit and matter
Wood
       through water and air

camphor eaglewood gutta-percha
home, names marked in memory

O kemuning, O waringin
O kemung, angsana, nangka
O gaharu and pauh hutan
O cendana, gemia, setar, celagi
O halban, bongor, ketengga

19

When the way prevails across the land
fleet-footed horses graze on the fields
When the way fails across the land
warhorses breed on the borders

Weapons are inauspicious vessels:
to glorify them is to exult in killing
Weapons are inauspicious vessels:
abide in them and lose everything

20

All under heaven say I'm vast, vast but like nothing
To be like nothing enables vastness
To be like this or that is to be but a speck of grain forever

There are three jewels I always embrace:
The first is called "compassion"
The second is called "restraint"
The third is called "unwilling to be first under heaven"
To be compassionate enables courage
To be restrained enables expansiveness
To be unwilling to be first under heaven enables the transfiguration of vessels

Now to give up compassion for courage, to give up restraint for expansiveness, to give up the last
        for the first is certain death
Through compassion prevail in war and strengthen the defenses
Heaven builds so as to build ramparts of compassion

21

When weapons reap profit, hope is left in the jar

Where troops once encamped, thorny brambles will grow

When two sides raise weapons in war, the sorrow-stricken will prevail

When one prevails in war, it is time to observe the funeral rites

22

Look at it and you can't see it
Listen to it and you can't hear it
Reach for it and you can't grasp it

Shapeless shape
Formless form
Ineffable image

To recognize the ancient origins
is called following the thread of the way

23

The way shatters and becomes vessels

The poet's employable and becomes tenured

Thus the uncarved block is ruined through usefulness

To realize its simplicity is to be freed of conceit

To be freed of conceit is to find fulfillment in stillness

24

Believable words are not beautiful, beautiful words are not believable
The wise are not learned, the learned are not wise
The virtuous are not excessive, the excessive are not virtuous
The poet hoards nothing—acts with respect toward others and gains more, gives all to others and
      gains still more
Thus the way of heaven benefits but doesn't harm, the way of humanity acts with dignity but doesn't
      contend

25

Nature eliminates excess and compensates for deficiency

26

Gaze in the grain
of worn wood, ghostly figures
hold another world

Impressions
of the unlived and unknown
pursue the real in the ideal
changes in the changeless

On the way to wholeness through concavity

27

Vastness means vanishing

Vanishing means distance

Distance means turning back

(Not knowing what is distant, look for it near at hand)

28

Langkha: "resplendent land"

    Sukkha: "bliss"

        Andrey

Platonov: *thus it is that bliss often lives unnoticed beside us*

29

At the ocean's center, the shadows tell us,
grows the life-giving tree Pauh Janggi
—the great coconut palm—
and beneath Pauh Janggi is a cave, Pusat Tasek,
the whirlpool navel of the waters
and inside the cave lives a giant crab
and when the crab emerges the tide rises
and when the crab returns the tide recedes

Janggi: Persian "zangi"; Ethiopian;
corr. to the East Coast of Africa;
"an adjective of remote or fabulous origin"

30

Syurga, heaven, exists above Pauh Janggi
Neraka, hell, exists below its roots

The gate to Neraka is guarded by a dragon
who possesses magic bezoar stones

Princess Siti Dewi, consort of Raja Seri Rama,
once sent Hanuman Ikan to borrow a bezoar
so as to cure a poisonous snake bite

31

A villager told Anker Rentse that the Kelantan
flood of 1926 swept a dragon with gold scales
out of a mountain cave
          The dragon plunged
into the Galas River and followed the floodwaters
down to Kuala Pergau, where it collided
with another dragon, one with silver scales,
and the two merged into one
          At Kuala Lebir,
this dragon collided with a third, steel-scaled dragon
and again the two merged into one
          The sea carried this dragon
all the way to Pusat Tasek
where they relieved their brother
as guardian to Neraka, for work in those days
was too hellish for one dragon

32

The shadows tell us how the Kelantan flood of 1926
happened: During the preparations for a grand feast
on the occasion of a circumcision, the beasts began to fight
one another—elephants against buffaloes, bulls against goats,
boars against cocks, and then, when a fight between
the cats and dogs broke out, a deluge poured down
from the mountains, drowning the people in the plains

Everyone drowned save a few villagers who had been gathering
firewood in the mountains, and the sun, moon, and stars
were extinguished, and darkness ruled the earth

When the light returned there was no land,
only sea as far as the eye could see, the flood
had spared no village, no habitation

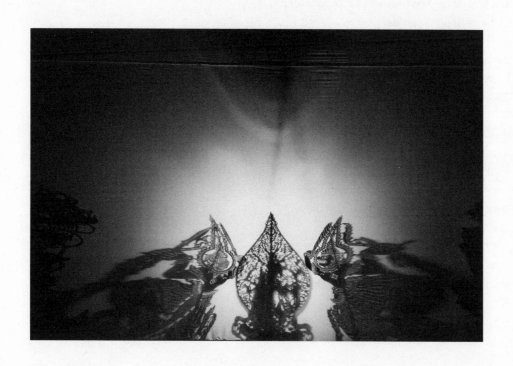

33

The Selk'nam tell of a time long ago when
their whole country flooded, the waters rising
so high the mountains were covered

      When people saw the great waters
coming, some ran out onto the rocks, some
turned into sea lions, others into birds
After the waters subsided, the sea lions
and birds stayed on the rocks and sandbanks,
as they still do to this day

      The Selk'nam say the flood happened
because the *xon*, or poets of those days, had not
been attentive to the rising waters soon enough
They should have stopped it and pushed it back

      Many years later, the great waters
threatened to flood their homeland again
This time the xon noticed it early and responded,
their attention focused and collected

      Practiced in their art, they gathered
together and joined the breath of their energy
against the force of the waters

      With so many moving xon, the waters
couldn't prevail—the flood could rise no more
and the people and animals survived unharmed

The *Hikayat Bayan Budiman* tales
told by a prescient parrot speak of a time
when the Golden Dragon arrived
at Pusat Tasek and all the monsters of the sea
tried to devour him. They caused such a ruckus
that Raja Naga, the serpent king, came out to see
what was happening. Raja Naga
then tried to swallow the Golden Dragon
three times but failed each time, so he seized
the Golden Dragon and slammed him
against the sea bottom, burying the dragon's head
into the bedrock. The little dragon, though,
didn't mind, and Raja Naga said to him,
"Speak the truth! *Titek deri pada
negri ninggua mana?* (From where have you fallen?)
Who gave birth to you?" The Golden
Dragon replied, "I have no nation nor kingdom,
no father nor mother, but I was incarnated
within the hollow of a bamboo stalk
the color of golden dust." When Raja Naga
heard this he sent for his *chermin mata* (eyeglasses)
and saw the real ancestry of the Golden Dragon.
He told him everything about his birth (*usul asal
ka-jadi-an-nya*), saying they were closely
related indeed, as the Golden Dragon's mother
was his sister. The serpent king kissed
and embraced his nephew, overjoyed
to have met him before his death,
for Raja Naga was old and ready to step
down from the throne. He summoned
a grand feast and *tabal* (crowned)
the Golden Dragon the new king.
Beloved by his uncle, the Golden Dragon
ruled Pusat Tasek through prosperity,
and with passing time, his *chula* (horn)
split into six heads making seven in all.

35

Jentayu (Garuda), Vishnu's bird,
lives in the branches of Pauh Janggi
When thick clouds suddenly block the sun,
people say, "Jentayu is spreading out his wings to dry"

The shadows speak of a time when Raja
Iskandar (Alexander the Great) set out to sail
to China to marry the Emperor's daughter
The Garuda-bird heard the news and flew
to tell Nabi Sulaiman (King Solomon)
Wholly disgusted at the thought
of a Muslim prince marrying an infidel,
he ordered Jentayu to stop the marriage by any means
        During Raja Iskandar's voyage to China,
Jentayu raised a storm that sank the ship
Everyone drowned save Raja Iskander
whom Jentayu grasped with his claws
and carried to Pusat Tasek
        There, Jentayu shut Raja Iskandar in a box
and tossed him into the whirlpool navel of the waters
But the current tore the box away from the whirl-
pool and it landed on the coast of China, whereupon
Raja Iskandar married the Emperor's daughter
        Word of this spread to Nabi Sulaiman
who raged and bellowed and condemned Jentayu
to the mountain Kaf (Caucasus) at the end
of the world for the rest of time

36

To find the camphor tree
you must learn its tongue

After many years of migration
seeking the end of the land
the two tribes journeyed farther and farther inland
driven from the sea borders toward
the center of the country where the province
policeman said primeval forests still exist
and where they could live unharmed by their fellow man
whom they feared more than the wild beasts

Though the two nations speak different languages
though one has black skin, the other light copper
though one has wooly hair, the other straight
though one had originally settled in the mountain jungles
and the other in the plains
they've lived peacefully with each other
guided by nomadic custom
prizing the freedom a hand-to-mouth
existence afforded them
      The two nations build no houses, believe
in no supreme deity, frequent no caves nor
sacred places, imagine no mythic
cause for thunder or lightning,
or sun, moon, or tides
      Their spirits live in the anthills
and their dead are buried on a log of wood
in a sitting posture, though adulterers
are often beaten with a club while asleep
then left to rot on open earth
      Polygamy is lawful but rarely practiced
A woman must agree on a marriage proposal
at which time the prospective husband
brings a gift of iron, or roots, or flowers
to her father and mother
      Their movements are graceful, bodies
lean and perfectly formed, eyes restless
anabasis, brought to the same place

It was in Kadaram, now Kedah,
as I explored the ruins of a Boudhist
temple, some distance from the sea
(an account of which I've yet
to send to the Asiatic Society of Calcutta)
where I found beneath a mound of sea-
shells locals call *kepah* and *karang*
a small coffeepot
carefully built of bricks
at a depth of four to five feet.
The lid was firmly baked
and upon handling the vessel
it crumbled to pieces. Within
stood the figure of a fowl
constructed of thin silver wire
which also fell to pieces as I
held it, but the bill and feet
remained unscathed, being made
of an alloyed metal, chiefly gold
in my hands, the emptiness
of the bird's presence left
me with a sweet melancholy.

39

There is the *jentayu*, never seen
but heard when the rains approach

The *chandrawasi* with no feet
live in the sea-foam or in the air
always on the wing
                                   It drops
its egg from the sky and when
the egg bursts close to earth,
fully fledged young fly out

A popular pantun proclaims:

> *Chandrawasi burong sakti*
> *Sangat berkurong didalam awan*
> *Gonda gulan didalam hati*
> *Sahari tidak memandang tuan*
>
> *Chandrawasi bird of power*
> *Enclosed in the clouds, hidden*
> *Anxiety reigns in my heart*
> *Each day I cannot see my love*

Pantun:
Old Javanese *tuntun* ("thread"), *atuntun* ("in lines");
Pampanga *tuntun* ("regular"); Tagalog *tonton* ("to speak
in a certain order"); Minangkabau *patuntun* ("guide")

40

There is a small bird called
burong tinggal anak, "goodbye children,"
who is heard when the padi rice sprouts
and as soon as her young hatch
she dies, singing, *"Tingal anak, tingal anak . . ."*
and the maggots from her corpse
feed her children

41

Eddin maps "a bouquet of names"
in his and Farish's *Spirit of Wood*

Lang-ya-hsiu, centered in Ligor,
linked to Kedah, "no doubt
an empire of some great extent"
under the suzerainty of the Funan Empire

Lanka in the *Ramayana* not Lankapuri
of Ceylon but Lankarkatyin of Ligor

Or further north, where Zheng He
charted Lang-I-chia in Pattani

That the *Nagarakretagama*, written
on palm leaves, mentions Lengkasuka,
a legend by the time of the Majapahit

Or was Kamalanga also Lang-ya-siu?
Or was it Lung-ya-hsü-chio, "place
without the azimuth"? Or sail six days and
six nights from Tan-ma-ling to reach
Ling-ya-ssi-kia?

Tripitaka Dharma Master Yijing notes
Lang-chia-shu being east of Criksetra

Or somewhere north of Singora,
bordering P'an-p'an, south of Dvaravati
today's Nakhon Si Thammarat?

Ko-lo at the Isthmus of Kra
Ch'ih-tu in Singora, Lo-yueh in Johore

During the Liang
the king of Tan-tan, northwest of To-lo-mo,
clad in the colors of the morning clouds
sends an envoy to the Chinese emperor
to request an interview with his most virtuous Majesty
—the one who steers government
in the kindness of the three treasures—
and offers these gifts: two ivory images, two pagodas,
fire pearls, *karpasi* cotton, and perfumes

South of Kedah, found
in the slab-graves of granite
cist, chronometry dates
from 1 to 7 AD:
Sixteen translucent dark-blue glass beads
A hexagonal biconical bead of rock crystal
Etched carnelian and agate beads
A fragment of light-green glass
Shards of earthenware pottery
Stone bark-pounder with crosshatching
Iron and bronze implements including
   a socketed iron tool *tulang mawas* used to chop timber
Bronze fragments with outwardly curling spiral spray row
   separated by herringbone pattern
Tang-era lead-glazed ceramic
Tang-era blackware
No traces of bone

43

The children stand in a row
staring straight ahead, hands
open behind their backs while
another child with a piece of wood
walks along behind them
touching their hands and chanting:

    chan chan siku rembat
    buah lalu di-b'lakang
    mata pějam tangan lihat
    siapa chěpat dia mělompat

        chan chan siku rembat
        the fruit passes behind you
        with eyes closed the hands see
        let the nimble one take the leap

Then the one with the wood fruit
in hand leaps away as the two
on either side stretch their legs out
to try and trip the one with the wood fruit
If she even gets touched, she is "it"
If he gets away, he goes to the end
of the playing field
and calls a child from the row
to come over and carry her back
to the others, where he stands before them
and is questioned:

Where do you come from? *(Datang dě'mana?)*
    I come from Kedah. *(Datang dě'Kedah.)*
What do you bring? *(Apa di-bawa?)*
    I bring a cooking pot. *(Bawa kuali.)*
Who is the master of the vessel? *(Siapa nakhoda?)*
    'Che 'Ali is the master. *(Nakhoda 'Che 'Ali.)*

Where is the boat you were towing? *(Mana sampan tunda?)*
        Parted from the rope. *(Putus tali.)*
Where is your pass? *(Mana pas?)*

And in reply the wood fruit is revealed
and both children rejoin the row

44

After the war, as the story goes,
Hanuman on the mountain peak
wrote the *Ramayana*, then scattered its pages
which floated into oblivion
but for one fragment Valmiki captured
and changed into ten thousand forms

45

Vastness without boundary
Real revealed as unreal

Square without corners
Vessel last to completion
Note of the rarest tone
Image without shape

Nameless way abundant

What centers the heart

46

It confers spirit upon the spirits

It is the granary of the ten thousand things

The ten thousand things
carry the Yin on their backs
and embrace the Yang in their arms
—the two energies reach a harmonious unity
with a third energy that emerges through vitality

It acts according to virtue
        nourishes the ten thousand things
        feeds them, perfects them
        crystallizes them, shelters them
and yet it claims no possession
It does great things, and yet does not boast of doing so
It makes things grow, and yet holds no authority over them

It is always inactive, and yet leaves nothing undone
        returns to the root of stillness in oblivion
        the surface of water at rest

47

Heaven and earth lack benevolence—
they treat the ten thousand things like straw dogs

As the poet, too, lacking benevolence
perfected in the way with ears keenly tuned
treats the ten thousand things like straw dogs

Straw dogs being offerings to the gods
prepared with reverence and mindfulness

Once the occasion has ended, they're tossed
into the street, trampled beneath passing feet

Indeed, the space between heaven and earth
is like a bellows—empty but inexhaustible
the more taken in the more comes into being

More and more words wholly exhausted
So much the better to observe emptiness

from which flows forth *al-nafas al-rahmaniy*
"the breath of the Merciful," Nature's being

In the beginning, God gave Gabriel
the Breath of Life to pass to Adam.
Adam's body was still lifeless earth
and water when the archangel flew
down to place the Breath by his nostrils
and animate him. But Gabriel, wanting
to see the Breath, opened his hands
and the Breath escaped, becoming
hantu, disembodied spirits, the older
siblings of humankind who dwell in darkness,
while the children of Adam live in the light
Invisible air and fire, sometimes envious,
and if accidentally disturbed, vindictive,
hantu are propitiated through the *main
peteri* rite. Some say the Breath went up
Adam's nostrils and he sneezed, scattering
the Breath across his body. His body was
too weak for the Breath, which broke
into little fragments. God told Gabriel
to weld (*peteri*) the fragments back together,
and so the *main 'teri* healing rituals weld
people together through play (*main*),
making sick people well. And the Wind,
the anthropologist said, blew inside her
own chest with the force of a hurricane.

49

Words heal through music,
gesture, the loop of cord

weld the pieces together

with the rhythm, the *tok 'teri-
minduk* song *bisik risik hidu*

      called *kramat*: sacred
      called *jampi*: incantation
      called *roh*: life spirit, breath, soul

Popped flowerbud rice medicine
falls to the palms of Fatimah
who plants the flower, the shoot
becomes Rama's Arrow Gandewat

. . . open the blocked gates of Wind

Wind as small as a sesame seed
Wind as small as a mustard seed
Wind called a golden bouquet of flowers
Wind called a silvery bouquet of flowers
Wind glows with five rays of light
Wind emerges with seven claps of thunder
      from the tip of eternity
        down through the generations
Wind beckoned by the father
Wind tended by the mother
Wind rules over a handful of earth, a drop
      of water
A drop of water, a tongue of flame
A puff of Wind watches over the world
      born from a split betel nut
Wind lands on the soil of Langkasuka
Winds that interpret our very souls, awake

50

    Who are you?
They call me Old Toddy Tapper
    Who are you?
They call me Fish Hanuman
    Who are you?
They call me Old Birdcatcher
    Who are you?
They call me Pak Deh
    Who are you?
They call me Old Will-o'-the-Wisp
    And you?
They call me Miss Ketuk-ketak

Spirits invited to the feast
gather in the audience chamber
as you weigh the words before speech
wending the way to the place

Of the blood sea and the heart field
words the real midwives of the ceremony

51

Of old those versed in the way
so finely subtle, so mysterious
in what was conveyed, too deep
to mark, too profound, and so
because they couldn't be marked
as known, they endeavored to say:

> As if intently wading (*breath*) through the waters in winter
> As if cautiously fearing (*breath*) the four neighbors
> Exacting (*breath*) like a guest
> Fragmenting (*breath*) like thick ice
> Unaffected like the uncarved block (*breath*)
> Unfiltered like turbid water (*breath*)
> Broad (*breath*) like a valley

The muddy, stilled, slowly turns clear
The settled, stirred, slowly gives birth
Those who preserve this way want no excess
and by wanting no excess achieve the worn and unfinished

52

The curator Mr. Wray said that
the people of Perak say the weaver-
bird wields a golden needle to make
its bottle-shaped nest. The nest
hangs from the branch of a low tree
in a swamp, a tree infested with red
ants or wasps, and if you carefully
pick the nest apart without
breaking a single piece of it,
you can find the needle. But if you
thoughtlessly pull it apart, if you
break even a single thread of grass
while unraveling its wondrous nest,
the golden needle will disappear.

53

Abolish the poet, abandon the sage:
People will profit one hundredfold

Abolish benevolence, abandon righteousness:
People will return to filial compassion

Abolish shrewdness, abandon profit:
Crooks and thieves will no longer exist

These three notions, deficient in writing,
need other affiliations to fall into place:

Manifest the plain, embrace the rough
Shrink the self, widow wants

Hundreds of mirrors circled Rama's waist;
thousands of mirrors circled his legs, across
the seams of his *beraduwanggi*, mirrors
sparkled down his body
   His belt of flowered cloth, twenty-five cubits
in length, or thirty with the fringe, changed colors
three times a day: transparent as dew in the morning,
midday a *lembayong* purple, evening dark as oil
   His velvet coat a dark magenta, brilliant
surface luster, like sunlight rippling on lake water
The dyer who made the coat sailed the world
for three years after making it, and still the dark dye
stained the palms of his hands
   His sarang of fine muslin
no ordinary weaving, stitched in a jar
in the middle of the sea by people with gills,
carried by others with beaks and, once finished,
its maker killed so that no one else could make one like it—
if put in the sun it grew damp, if soaked in water it dried;
if torn, its mended darning only increased its value,
the thread so rare a single dewdrop could tangle it
for the length of a cubit, while the breath
of the south wind could disentangle it
   The straight blade of his dagger grooved
retak mayat, started from its base to the damask
pamur janji halfway up, to the damask *lam jilallah*
at the point, and there, parallel with the edge, the *alif*
edge ended where the steel turned white:
"This blade no ordinary steel, made from the leftover
material of God's Ka'abah bolt, forged by the son
of God's prophet, Adam, smelted in the palm of his hand,
fashioned with the end of his finger, colored with the juice
of flowers in a Chinese furnace, its fatal attributes
descended from the sky, so that if cleaned at the source
of a river, the fish at the *embouchure* floated belly-up"

The sword he wore *lang pĕn-gonggong*,
the successful swooper, a kite carrying off its prey;
his handkerchief *dĕndam ta'sudah*, endless love,
knotted with projecting ends, remained unfinished,
for if it were ever finished, it would bring the end
of the world; its cloth woven in no ordinary way,
made by his mother in her youth, giving it all its love-
compelling secret names
    In this way Rama set forth on his journey,
adopting the art of *sedang budiman*, the young snake
that writhed at his feet, his shadow at midday,
a young eagle soared on the wind overhead;
he took one step forward and then two backward: one
forward as a sign of him leaving his country, two backward
as a sign he'd return; his right step caused his left-
side equipage to clang, his left step caused his right-side
equipage to clang; he advanced by swelling out his broad
chest, and letting his slender fingers drop, adopting the gait
called "planting beans," then the step "sowing spinach"

55

Not knowing when to stop from fullness the valley runs dry

Not knowing when to stop from profit leaders fall

And so profit's root is the humble, as the base of the high is the low

What is the humble as root?

Wanting neither the riches of jade nor the hardness of stone

And thereby endure

56

Somewhere in the borderland forest
a mouse deer springs from a pool

a blade flashes with borrowed sunlight
the acanthus burns in the flame of the wood

I was there and not there, listening
to the insects hum *belum-balam belum-balam*

the palm blossoms weep with remembering
the singing and clapping to serunai, gong, drum

I was aware and not aware of the whirlwind,
the echo, the words waived out of air and

fire, the hantu spirits cooled with rice seeds
mixed with salt and soot, assam and turmeric,

sprinkled between floorboards, earth to earth,
water to water, I could see and not see

the roofs thatched with hair, walls of skin,
posts shaped from the heart of the nettle tree,

round amber eyes watching me watching
me, cross the first pool into the middle

(a ripple of wind skims the surface of the water)

cross the second pool out of the fold

(a diver's face rises to the surface of the water)

semangat like a bird on the wing inside me
drawn through the hidden ways of the wood

as nāga rotates around the earth
and the moon rides the tiger

Maharaja Wana, King of Demons, dreams
of an old woman who tells him
that a human king is building a causeway
bridge to his country, Langkasapuri.
Maharaja Wana—red face, bulging
nose, sharp teeth, clawed hand grasps a cudgel,
royal ring on the pinky of the other hand,
arm articulated, fiery pinnacle crown of faces
atop his head—wakes anxious and fearful, claws out.
He hurries to consult his astrologer, Mah Babu Sanam,
his youngest brother, who divines
that the dream is true, and Seri Rama, incarnation
of Vishnu, the king. "Hardly unexpected,"
Mah Babu Sanam says to his brother, "given your actions—
first kidnapping his mother [aside: *actually her double*],
and then his wife [aside: *no doubt his daughter*]."
Maharaja Wana throws a fit, refuses to believe
the truth, tramples and kicks his brother,
banishes him to the sea. Mah Babu Sanam—
trimmed beard and mustache, eyes calm, *tengkolok*
headdress, carved crutch raised in his motionless hand,
painted cowhide palm turned up in a plea for mercy—
is eventually found by Hanuman Kera Putih.
He agrees to join the White Monkey
to help Seri Rama defeat the King of Demons,
Tuan Puteri Mata Api—his daughter
with the burning eye-beams—the seven Pari
princesses, and the rest of the demon's crew.
The blue-green king is victorious, flashes
pataka mudra, and enthrones Mah
Babu Sanam as the ruler of Langkasapuri.

58

Seri Rama says, "It was the magic gem
Batara Guru gave me that protected us
from the burning gaze of Tuan Puteri Mata Api.

And the masked *jembalang* Pari princesses, *lah!*
—those spirits can possess you and crack
your mind, but the monkey warriors prevailed."

59

When Maharaja Wana defeated Sirat
Maharaja, Seri Rama's father, in the upper
world, he claimed Cahaya Bulan as his wife.
"Go to hell," Sirat Maharaja wheezed
unequivocally through his wounds. "Please,
my darling," Cahaya Bulan entreated,
"we must do as the demon says. I go willingly."
The queen retired to the palace pool
to bathe, and there, with the assistance of the gods,
she rubbed the dirt from the pores of her body
and shaped the dirt into her double, Madudaki.
"I am as beautiful as you," Madudaki cooed.
Cahaya Bulan pointed to the door:
"Go now and fulfill your duty." Madudaki
slowly blinked, and left the upper world
with Maharaja Wana. She became the queen
of Langkasapuri. When their daughter was born,
Madudaki secretly placed the baby in a vessel
made of wood and sent her down the river,
into the forest (some say Mah Babu Sanam
sealed the fetus in a jar and threw it in the ocean).
She was found by the sage Maharisi.
He raised the child as his own daughter,
the one known as Siti Dewi, Seri Rama's love.

60

The demon disguised himself
as a golden barking deer to lure

his daughter from their ashram
Moonlight fled through the trees

Siti Dewi chased the illusion—
the mellifluous bleats of the deer

familiar, the way the deer's skin
shimmered like *ton-byan* finery

until she was caught
by her demon father

and carried through the air
to Langkasapuri, Jentayu felled

Why is the tip of Hanuman Kera Putih's tail
red? Because Maharaja Wana soaked him in oil
and set him on fire, and the White Monkey,
born of the wind, leapt onto the palace roof
and on from roof to roof of the houses,
spreading the fire through Langkasapuri.
He laughed and whirled in the air, his body
untouched by the fire except for the tip
of his tail, where the flame burned and
burned. Hanuman howled; the kingdom
blazed. No matter how hard he thrashed
his tail, no matter how much dirt he piled
on it, the flame still burned, even underwater.
Then Sirat Maharaja from the upper world
shouted down, "Put your tail in your mouth!
That will do the trick!" And so Hanuman
stuck his tail in his mouth—the fire snuffed
out but left the red tip, forever marked.

Pak Dogol, incarnation of Dewa
Sang Tunggal, god above all gods,
greater than Shiva, most humble
and ugly clown, the original shadow
master, covered with mud,
disguised as Rama's servant, bald
head, two teeth, beak nose, round
body shaped after a certain tomb-
stone seller in Kampung Mentuan,
palang knife in hand, sarang tied
to his waist, loose trousers, the one
who found Siti's eyes when Mahajara
Wana stole them, the one who felt
lonely on earth and formed
a soul from his own body's dirt,
but ran out of dirt before finishing
all his fingers. Called Wak Long, Pak
Dogol's sidekick, intermediary
between worlds, dalang's trance
body, messenger, improviser,
laughs and says, "The *wayang*
is like a magic mirror that
reflects our lives but leaves
out the details in such a way
for its essence to shine forth."

63

Tree of life in the leaf
animals, flowers, vines

birds in the sky, peak

spirit
          flame, *pohon*
beringin, banyan
tree, elephants in the leaf

sway the colors in shadow
skin against cloth, mountain

alam, world lengthens,
swells and warps, returns

layers to underworld handle

returns, life tree
to the banana stem
stillness, shadows

return
          to the shadowlight stillness

Offerings of jasmine flowers, betel
leaves and nuts, rolled cigarettes, coins,

cotton thread, yellow, parched,
turmeric rice, sown on the bodies
dispelled

Gong opens the roof
Wall of the world rises

smoke from the lamp to the sun

        dust and deities rise

Shadows
        visible non-
        material spirit
rest in the words

demigods of the bows

rest
canang and tetawak
        gongs, silent
drums, serunai
silent

        wind
        holds the five pillars

dalang and gamelan

rest in the rice-paste
kemenyan incense, pinang fan

        After the feasting of the spirits
        After the water pot is broken

flowers and leaves scatter
the seven dancers and five musicians

All depart into safety
in silence and peace

        after the ancestors return
the generations
           return
through the estuary world

Rest in the wind
      stone, wordless way

      sleep, waves
rest in the wind

      shadows
           play

for Eddin Khoo and Pauline Fan

and in memory of Carol Laderman (1932–2010)
and Din Cheuk Lau (1921–2010)

II

Line and Light

1

Ceiling turned to sky

Time to timelessness

Further from the center to the outer stations, along darkening tracks along opposing banks

Through the fjord the sound, river iced over

Night valley emptiness, seawater tide, shored

Against wreckage, for a new form to live by

Runs the line, out, on and ahead, reaching toward, into

Now held by the light of the end, here

Of what was and to come, past the storm-cloud mountain

City of broken glass, circle of boulders, lightning-rod field

Scholar-rock memory, floating gate in the middle sea: eagle-shadow, tower break-

Water, frozen fragments, cracking sheet, silence of life beneath

Wind swirls the snowgrains, echoes raised in the breath, the pause

Fading moon at the last quarter, wild grass not dead but asleep

Steady iamb of freight cars from the other side, breaking free

Island apart, between, negative halo hovering

Moment, of the radiant spheres, burning asterisks

2

Darkness goes to dawn as the lights fade and the lines appear, formless shadows beginning to shape the nature of surroundings.

Poles set horizontally across the meridian would make it appear to be a construction site, or a cage, from a distance, recognizable screen.

But with space between the lines the evidence of what was extant merges into the clouds of the mind as different signals or signs.

Morning's ordinary stillness: listening for the horses-of-the-Frisians lapping the waves, hearing the crosstalk of autumn birds.

The flute of the orchards brightening blue, the way whitecaps play against a barge drifting slowly toward the remembered city.

Time reverses in the golden light, the reds and yellows blur the frame into a postcard signed "Love, M. M."

Everything was made to matter—out of spirit.

Seventeen echoing a hidden significance when measured against the proportions of the collapsing structure.

Even now, following this track of influence and arriving on the little island, overgrown, wild with green plants and trees, plastic chairs, rubble, beer cans, new metal reinforcements against a history of natural destruction.

Above the grottoes and cisterns the vertical screams.

Set in a former room by the former stairs spiraling topography into air.

How sight follows the real, hollow becomes hub, cave an inner exaltation.

Noble deer, swimming toward the island in the summer rain, when lightning was a god's fury, hidden gods, of forest and current, *tawhid* oneness in unity, what hoped for fidelity, in the absence, along the bone-scattered shore, hart's ribcage, red-winged trill.

Vines cling to the mortar binding the crumbling brick wall.

River-moat provided safety and protection to the castle arsenal, built with cement and junk sealing brick, cannonball ornaments, rope-patterned juttings, brushwood burner atop corbelled cylinders, capstan and sally ports, ramparts to pilasters, finial buoys on buttresses, steps to wee bay, Gatling guns on sunporches, now portcullis emptiness, powdered memory of a flint economy hosting new wars.

Picturing facts: exposed juniper berries, voices of hikers descending, water celery swaying in the shallows, inert stones, the painted lines blending into translucent spheres, gesturing before that, before that . . .

Their points of interrelation cannot manifest themselves but in the artifact that swells and glows.

3

Last light dims to first light

Standing on a platform looking through the dusk

At the *holi* fire-yellow dusting the brae branches like corn pollen

Sprinkled in curving rows and spirals of a hidden truth

The passing names, imagined lines, what exists as a renewed sense of place

Night, day, night rhythm of architectonic projection

Darkness slowly deepening with filaments igniting, one by one

Translating the sun, each luminous body filling the space within it

One pause, then another, listening to a *beehive of light* switch on

Seeing the island as if from the other side of a celestial mirror

As if these same words were already written but with different meanings

On a slope shadow of a cypress rising out of nothingness into the open

Against the distant lights of the houses, each point at rest locates its fullest intensity

Unaware at the time this was an emblem of happiness

Moths circling the glass, nature dissolves the mind

How conquest becomes decay, disrupting the perimeter

Of the constellation: line and light, figure and void

Ceiling and Time

10

The stars inside preside
over time, for a century

now you've passed through
the viaduct vestibule, followed

the passageways to the signs
and tracks, arrived, left, as if

guided by the gods, head
down, lines set with little

fear of being transformed
into a bird, or a mountain

14

Under the Uranometric sky I

have on occasion emerged out
onto the busy concourse to be

struck by the sunlight fenestrata
of the shadows and beams, wings

beating between ceiling and time,
the axial order, conversant lines

What lasts in an age of planned
obsolescence? Who blasted rock

and earth, submerged the steel
forest, raised the Doric stylobate?

What beauty commutes in the grand
design? Pegasus, Musca, Caen stone

repro? And the galleries that embrace?

14

Aragon arcades *aquarium humain*, crowded
novelties bought, sold, refuge from rain

Ghostly substrate of our virtual aerarium
glory or scourge of the age, world-image

Down the ramps to the ballroom or roller
disco, ramp after ramp branching down in-
to the underground, platforms at standstill

down, farther down the alluvium depths
past the sliding gates, nameless archways,

banks of wires and levers, rails below girders,
broken schist marine layers, mailroom switch-
boards boiler battery hatch ladder basement

yard, down the substation powerhouse, rotary
ruin, generators and rectifiers, terminal grace

5

Double row of half-moon windows
clerestory floats on water of the sea

Ecliptic crosses the equatorial, winter
fades into obliquity, above the workaday

station's living pace, transitory space

7

Giant chandeliers droop down, alloyed
halos of eggs, auratic, hollowed nothing-

ness fluorescence illuminates acorn and leaf

Botticino marble dado, pose and snap,

tap to send, share, post in the architecture

where ants and rats search dark cracks
for crumbs, tastes insatiable for waste

4

Careened down the double staircase
and barreled into rush hour—Roger

tripped, broke a rib, his doctor assured
him, "Don't worry, that rib's a spare"

8

She stood beside the opal clock
at the pagoda node, texting next

to a tall, oval object encased in cloth,
while the suited rubberneck waves

hurried by—her inamorata appeared

They smiled, pecked, gestured, each
lifted an end of the object overhead

: skylit trilithon crossed terrazzo sea

10

Missed the late train by seconds
Chic bar closed at the entresol

Cast off the steps by a guard, sat
on a pink stone slab, back to wall,

half-drunk, caught between ceiling
and time, excess and need, silence

and plea: *Climb down from the roof-*
top Mercury, and lend me your talaria,

Minerva, show me what Tiresias saw
for you to bestow the gift of the birds

10

Shoe shiner next to flower seller circle
magazine stands, plastic snacks, black

ladies in blue liveries, dressing maids,
toiled for the beatification of moneyed

patrons, colorless faces at the Carrara

glass salon, separate room for immigrants
laborers, infrastructured social relations, a

public space: browse razors, lotions, watches,
lob moon balls on the fourth-floor tennis court

before the slow arc home back to station wages

2

Neither shinkansen nor maglev metal mastodons
lumbering through the snows, switch frog-croaks

14

Every monument contains its forgetting

Baths of Caracalla demolished across town

Where will you sleep with no home to go to?

You who have awakened from many dreams

descending the slope toward the empty
food court, under the low herringbone

arches and Guastavino tiles, listening to
far-off voices whisper along the walls,

What we call progress is imprisoned on every earth,
and fades away with it, Blanqui from eternity

And you, will you make it to the last departure?

Ruins reborn in their own memories, bays,
Corinthian columns, operatic balconies *de la*

Cité church stable hospital orphanage erased

2

Time sighs, "You aspire and expire"
Ceiling hides, "Nothing's forever"

For Ahmatjan Osman, in the absence

Stones and Stars

There's a cemetery near my home that belongs to a state prison, inherited from the "hospital for the criminally insane" that the prison used to be. It lives quietly behind the local high school, between the tennis courts and the new football field, hidden by tall pines and maples and other trees. A barrier gate with private-property signs, piled dirt, is easily skirted round the middle of the overgrown path continuing on to the cemetery. The path runs along a chain-link fence, arms emptied of wire, dividing a row of residential houses on the left and the cemetery on the right. The cemetery rests in an air of secrecy and seclusion, as if it belongs somewhere else, deep in the forest, or in another era or dimension or trance, accident or afterthought, though it still happens to exist here, in this time and place, a diurnal sphere of the latitude's changing seasons.

The prison is only a stone's throw up the main road from the high school, so that one must pass the high school when walking from the prison to the cemetery, or if walking from the cemetery to the prison. The high school was built just after the turn of the second millennium, over a century after the prison hospital opened. Part of the prison hospital complex eventually turned into a separate prison, and then a "correctional facility" for women. This prison, with its greenhouses, fill-up station, handball wall, barns, buildings lining an inner hexagonal courtyard, was shuttered a decade after the high school opened and remains abandoned in a field, waiting for capital development pitched to the state. A path along the western edge of the cemetery leads out beyond the football field, through the abandoned prison field to the open prison.

The graves in the prison cemetery are small, wedge-shaped footstones that bear no names. The stones are arranged in roughly spaced rows. The same cross appears mechanically carved in relief on the inclined face of each stone, while a different, four-digit number (or a combination of letters and numbers) is engraved on the bottom, vertical edge of each stone. Some of the stones with crosses are numberless, blank. The older, weathered stones look like granite; the newer ones, fewer in number, look like cement. The sphere of the cemetery is divided into two spheres: the western stones face east, the eastern stones face west. A smaller, separate, third sphere of stones north reflects stars instead of crosses, though the crosses outnumber the stars by many, many stones. These stones with stars face south in one long, runover line, flush left.

Three of the stones with stars bear a stainless-steel plaque shaped like a military dog tag embossed with a name, number, and dates. No stones face north, toward the prison. The living do not visit this place to remember the dead shielded by stones, crosses, stars. The prison cemetery is barred from the living while not barring the living from visitation. Listening for the smallest voice in the sheltered air, hushed asylum. Some of the stones have shifted, sunken, turned in the earth, migrant tilt, the dead restless underground. Grass green in sun shadow lush clumps of blade and bract stems honeysuckle blooms. Two rows of hemlocks marked with a giant white "X" on each trunk divide the spheres. What masks the living, binds the dead? Needles weep, breathe our breath above upturned grass and earth, freshly filled graves, a deer eating forbs among the stones.

III

No Home Go Home
Go Home No Home

家なき家に帰る
帰る家のない家

Drawings by Kazumi Tanaka
Japanese Translations by Hiroaki Sato

Note

When I first visited Kazumi Tanaka's studio in a renovated brick building at the end of a small bridge above a creek in our town, she showed me a series of tea-ink drawings she had been working on since 2007, each image brushed on a ten-by-ten-inch paper sheet and connected to a particular memory of her Osaka childhood. Kazumi had expected the pictures to fade gradually with time, turning the weeks and months she had spent on each drawing into a meditation on temporality and evanescent memory. She stored the drawings carefully, rarely bringing them out into the light, and as time passed, the images showed no signs of vanishing, the umber lines and shades even deepening against the pale-yellow paper.

Kazumi displayed the drawings for me on a table, each work covered with a square sheet she flipped, like the pages of a book, to reveal the picture underneath, and then covered it again before moving on to the next one. The order of the drawings seemed deliberate, the kinds of tea leaves used for each drawing varied, subject to chance and experiment. The small scale of the work and the act of turning each sheet to view the next image heightened the intimacy of the experience. The detailed simplicity and finely measured strokes, the shifts in perspective and distance, the repetition of certain ritual objects, the specificity of the flowers, the changing position of the drawing on the page that usually occupied a section of the square field—all of these aspects spoke to the work's art, an art that reminded me of the double-leaf butterfly mounting of the classical Chinese album.

Small, delicate, portable—the Chinese album merged poetry, calligraphy, and painting into a serial practice of reading and seeing. Thought to have originated during the Tang dynasty as Buddhist sutras were being translated and passed around, the traditional album consisted of a sequence of images on a single, or mixed, subject such as flowers, birds, animals, human figures, bamboo, or views of a landscape—the world encompassed in the world's particulars. The painter and writer Shitao (1642–1707) made a lasting contribution to the art form. Shitao, or Daoji, cousin of the "mad monk" painter Bada Shanren (one of his seals, we are told, read "control madness"), lived most of his life through the transition of the Ming to the Qing in the seventeenth century as an itinerant Buddhist monk and painter. Shitao believed personal belongingness involved "an absolute sense of place" and embraced the concept of the single brushstroke as the origin of all phenomena: "Mountains, rivers, and I merge in spirit and meld into a single line."

Shitao's innovative album *Returning Home* is part of the collection at the Metropolitan Museum of Art in New York. Twelve paintings are paired with twelve poems, alternating images of flower and plants with landscape views, while the calligraphic style of each poem changes according to the content and style of the paintings, or the style of painting changes according to the style of calligraphy, vermillion seals harmonized with the design. A tiny wash of color doesn't appear until the fifth leaf, on the face of the lonely traveler, squinting from the cold in a skiff. Sometimes a poem only fills a small portion of a leaf; other times it fills half a leaf or the full leaf. Shitao made the album at a tumultuous point in his life. Born to a Ming imperial prince who was killed trying to claim the throne when Shitao was only four, he took Buddhist vows to avoid persecution in the newly-established Manchu state. After living almost forty years as a monk, he made the journey to Beijing to accept the honor of a second audience with Emperor Kangxi. He failed to attain imperial patronage and quickly became disillusioned with the "floating world" of the capital. A "tenfold bitter coldness" overwhelmed him as he made his way home south to Yangzhou in 1692. He would make his album in late 1695, during another period of wandering. "With respect to antiquity," Shitao asks, "how could I have learned from it without transforming it?" He left the sangha a year or two later to devote himself entirely to his art as a secular Daoist and teacher.

After that initial encounter, words and lines surfaced in my mind out of Kazumi's drawings. Thoughts bound to no single narrative, no single theme, image opening a way into a world of connotations wheeling around the icon of home as presence and absence. Worried I would be using her private childhood memories and dreams for my own nefarious sanctifications, I asked Kazumi how she felt about the possible conjunction of words with her pictures. Instead of spitting in my face she encouraged me to continue. We talked more about the drawings and her family history. Was there a way to conceptualize the drawings the way Tōru Takemitsu conceptualized the water dreaming in that Papunya painting? Could the poems be a gift to the drawings the way poetry is a gift to words? What transubstantiated through the writing formed a loose renga, using Kazumi's pictures as a visual linkage between each verse—each image a verse unit—so that the end of one poem foretells the image that follows it while each poem dwells on the image before it. As with Shitao's album, the drawings and poems of our little book look for a paradoxical way home, when return is an impossibility.

At the heart of No Home Go Home / Go Home No Home is Kazumi's mother, a longtime devotee of Tenrikyo, a religion strongly influenced by Shintoism and Buddhism. Only a few decades younger than Mormonism, Tenrikyo originated in the nineteenth century through the teachings of a peasant woman, Nakayama Miki, whose revelations of Tenri-O-no-Mikoto are recorded in her Ofudesaki (Tip of the Writing Brush). Tenrikyo tells us that the body is a thing lent, a thing borrowed from God the Parent, and so through hinokishin, or daily service, one can awaken the divine intention within and attain the Joyous Life.

Divine intention. Divine transposition: what the illustrious dice-throwing French poet of a distant century felt to be the "spiritual task" of poetry in its movement from fact to ideal through the apperception of relations and vital rhythm, "each soul a melody renewed." Master Hiroaki Sato, generous and melodic soul, has contributed the Japanese translations to the poems to complete the album's circle—home-no-home, from line to image to line, crossing the ocean back to the place of the Mother's tongue. Not long after we completed the album, Kazumi's mother passed away and her house in Osaka—the house Kazumi grew up in, the house you see here—was bulldozed. Whatever ideal of the whole the poem still reaches for, whatever transposition of language and experience and vision, endures through the memory space of shadows and light, here set in traces of tea and ink, pictures and words.

The song　　　　brought me to a far place

And suddenly　　I　　was back home

Without having noticed　　　　my return

歌が　　遠いところにわたしを連れてきた

そして突然　わたしは　うちに戻っていた

気づかぬままに　　　　　わたしの帰郷

[*Nest*. 10 x 10 inches. Irish breakfast tea on paper.]

Where do you come from?   Where did you grow?   Your leaving brought you here

to the nest at the center of your home   Where have you flown?   Your lowered

gaze meets the angle of light   its just-made-ness   awaits   the songbird's

return   circle of twigs and air   shadow halo   against the nothing mirror

Does the charcoal branch still burn   in the iron brazier   beneath

the moonfaced kettle   embraced by the trivet?   Little eyes of a fish rise up

through the water   heat   leaves steep   ink   pools   brush-

stroke memory   On a square patch of earth   breathes in   emptiness

between the pale yellow glow   outside   and the native   house

どこから来るのか　　　　　　　どこで育ったのか　　　　　　去ったのでここに来た

家の真ん中の巣　　　　どこから飛んできたのか　　　　　　　お前の見下ろす

凝視は明かりの角に会い　　　　その出来たばかりの　　　　囀り鳥の　戻りを

待つ　　　　小枝と空気の円　　　　　　影の円光　　　　　　無の鏡を背に

炭枝は　　　　　　　　鉄火鉢の中で　　　　　　月のように丸顔の薬缶の

下で　　　五徳に包まれてまだ燃えるのか　　　　　魚の小さな目が　　水の中を

上がり　　　　　熱　　　葉は浸る　　　墨　　溜まり　　　筆

遣い記憶　　　　　　四角の地面に　　　　　吸い込む　　　　空

薄黄色の光　　　　　　　　と外側　　　　　と土地の　　　　　家

[*House*. 10 x 10 inches. Ti kuan yin (oolong) tea on paper.]

The garden path begins   at the southeast corner   behind   the wooden fence

that bends from the vertical edge   nearer you   into sunlight   drawn

abode of vacancy   a   skyful   nostalgia   washes over the heart

That longing to open the gate   step   inside   and walk   into spring

She appeared to the poor farmer in a dream   kuanyin iron spirit   of the shrine

he had tended   through so many seasons   she led him to the cave   to the

buried root   merciful shoot   passed on   leaves   to brew

a temporary refuge   gateless gate   What's perceived   in the

recollection   shrinks   Roof tiles   inhale the wind   from the inumaki

pine   you see   it grows   in me   Time's   displaced embrace

Utility pole   sends its signals   over the low eaves   Who is the one

gazing out of the window   beyond the garden   faceless   face?

庭の小道が始まる　　　　　　　　　東南の角　　　　　木板の塀の　　　　　後ろ

縦の角から曲がり　　　　　君に近づき　　　　　　　陽光に　　　　　引かれる

空き地の住処　　　　空一杯　　　　　の　　　　　郷愁　　　　　が心をよぎる

かの門を開く憧れ　　　　　一歩　　　　　入り　　　　　歩く　　　　春の中に

彼女は夢に貧しい農夫に現れ　　　　　　　　　　　　社の　　　　　観音鉄の意気

男が世話をした　　　いく星霜　　　　　女は男を洞に導き入れ　　　　　埋めた

茎に　　　　慈悲満ちた木の芽　　　　手渡す　　　　葉々を　　　　　煎じる

束の間の隠れ家　　　　　　無門関　　　　　感知されるもの　　　　思い出の

中　　　　　　縮む　　　　屋根瓦　　　　風を吸い　　　　　犬槇

松　　　ほら　　　　成長する　　　わたしの中で　　時間の　　行き場なき抱擁

電柱　　　　信号を送る　　　　　低い軒端の上を　　　　　誰だあの

窓から眺め　　　　　　庭の彼方の　　　　　　　　　顔なき　顔は

87

[*Girl*. 10 x 10 inches. Oolong tea on paper.]

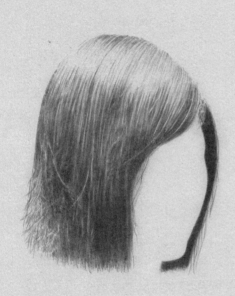

To arrange the stones   at the fountain basin   close your eyes   and scatter them

Water   drops   ring out   underground   slow   fast   slow   nature's

koto   Listening   to the silence   of the girl   her close-up quietness   nō

face   nō eyes   nō nose   nō mouth   only her hair   shines

with emptiness   figuring her presence   in the plant   that must

wither   under sun   before it can release   the dragon

Freshly cut   bob   combed   wave to   streaked strands   more

alive than flesh   fades   strand   by strand   What spirit   resides

in your hair?   Kami deity   where the eightfold clouds rise   with vitality

Who are you   ingrained in the cells?   Singing a song of the East   though

still in the land of the West   Encoding markers   making memory

open the garden gate   to face   a sunflower   inflorescence

噴水盤で　　　　　　石を並べるよう　　　　　目を閉じ　　　　　散らせ

水　　　滴が　　響く　　地下　　ゆっくり　速く　ゆっくり　自然の

琴　　少女の　　沈黙に　　聞き入る　　　　大写しの静寂　　　能

面　　　能目　　能鼻　　能口　　髪のみが　　　　光る

空に　　　　その存在を考え　　　陽のもとに　　　萎える

に違いない　　　　植物の中で　　　龍を　　　放つ前に

新鮮に切った　　　　短髪　梳かれ　縞入りの房　に波打ち　肉より

生き　　薄れ　房　　房ごとに　　いかなる精神が　あなたの髪に

宿るのか　　　神　　　八雲立つ　　　躍動

あなたは誰　　　　細胞に組み入られ　　　東方の歌を歌い　ながら

西方の地にいる　　　　　標識を解き　　　記憶を作る

庭門を開き　　　向日葵に　　　面す　　　花房

[*Sunflower*. 10 x 10 inches. Sabbathday Lake Shaker chamomile tea, green tea, Earl Grey tea on paper.]

Himawari fields   at Fukushima   absorb the poisons   of our ways

prone to blindness   and accident   known consequences   living

toward disaster   We are at the crisis point of the world   Tamijūrō Kume says

before his death   in the Kantō earthquake   1923   Turns to sun

we drink   its full bloom   nest   of a hundred flowers   in one

whorl   disk and ray   bursts forth   in happiness

and recurring beauty   summer's procession   ablaze

Tiny hairs   on its stem   scent of green   bracts   florets attract

gently wave   "Be . . . *like* me!"   they say   with unassuming simplicity

Cretaceous activity   flowering   anthers   in the balance   pollen-

charged legs   lighter than air   finds the style   hidden ovules   seeds

renew   Strong roots   grow down   into   the inner room

向日葵畑　　　　　　福島　　　　　　われらのやり方の　　　　　　毒を吸収する

盲目　　　　　　と事故になりがち　　　　　　予知できる結果　　　　　　災難の方に

生きる　　　　　　われらは世界の奇禍点にある　　　　　　と久米民十郎がいう

一九二三年　　　　　　関東大震災の　　　死の前　　　　　　陽に向かい

飲む　　　　　　そのま盛り　　　　　　百花の　　　　　　巣

一つ　　　　渦　　　　盤と光線　　　　　　爆ぜる幸福

繰り返す美　　　　　　夏の行列　　　　　　燃立つ

小さな髪の毛　　　　　　茎の上　　　　緑の香り　　　苞葉　　小花が惹く

優しく波　　　　「私の様に . . . なって!」　　　　　　と言う　　　　　　気取らぬ簡素さ

白亜紀の活動　　　　　　花咲く　　　　　葯　　　均衡取れた　　　花粉で

充ちた脚　　　　　　空気より軽く　　　　花柱を見つけ　　　　隠れた　　胚珠

新生　　　　　　強い根が　　　　奥の間　　　　　　に　生え下がる

95

[*Family Altar.* 10 x 10 inches. Houji tea on paper.]

Things lent   or   borrowed: your life   your   body   Crawl

through the passage   into the room   You approach   the gohonden

with offerings of sake   fruit   grain   raised on earth   altar   brings

harmony to the home   Before the butsudan   kamidana shrine   toko-

noma alcove   up three steps   to the ship of the seven gods   purifying

sakaki branch   landing point leaf   tip   of the brush   where the dragon

takes flight   Edges   blur   bleed into   an inner   nothingness

Braided rope   talismans hang down   cleansing testimony   between

portraits   and ancestral tablets   empty space   for the kami to dwell in

Will the proof-amulet   protect the remembrance?   Will the remembrance

be enough for the letting go?   Mother   moon and sun   musubi   life-

giving creativity   generative energy   reconnects   here   and there

Nō knowing   whom you may meet   in a dream   hitherto   hereafter

wisp   of steam   taste   of the sweet   strawberry shortcake

貸したり　　　借りた　　もの　　あなたの命　　あなたの　　　身体　　通路を

這い　　　　部屋に入る　　　　　　あなたは近づく　　　　　　御本殿に

酒のお供え　　果物　　　穀類　　　　地上で育てた　　祭壇は　　家に

和をもたらす　　　　仏壇の前に　　　　　　　神棚　　　床の

間　　　三段上がり　　　　七福神の宝船　　　　　清める

榊の枝　　　触る先の葉　　　　　先　　筆の　　龍が

飛び上がる　　　端が　　　薄れ　　内の　　無に　　滲みいる

編んだ綱　　　　お守りが垂れ下がる　　　清めの証言　　　肖像の

と先祖の位牌　　　　との間　　　空間　　　神が住む

証拠守りは　　　　　　記憶を守るか　　　　　　記憶は

放下に十分か　　　　母　　　月と日　　　結び　　命

与えの創造性　　生成的エネルギー　　結び直す　　ここ　　とあそこ

能知らぬ　　あなたが会うかもしれぬ人　　夢の中　　今まで　これから先に

湯気の　　一条　　味　　　甘い　　苺のショートケーキ

[*Cake.* 10 x 10 inches. Green tea, hibiscus tea, peppermint tea on paper.]

One foreigner   prisoner of war   turned the spit for a cake   in Nihon

island   This no baumkuchen   floating   strawberry cloud   childhood

I walk   through the layers   of the Miya mandara   at the foot of Mount Mikasa

moon full   above   a dip in the shadow-paper hills   and higher the five

avatars   watch over the forest scene   Jizō Bosatsu among them   sky mother

earth womb   waiting   at the river crossing   Everyone's asleep   save

the deer   prancing together outside the torii gate   A path   leads to a bridge

disappears in mist   suyari gasumi glimpse   of bare branches   translucent trunks

ghostly mounds   silver-white   blossoms   pink   faint lichen-green   dream

serene   bending stream   Path reappears   breaks off   temple   tilted

square   bird's eye view   facing East   memory's   sacred space   Empty

rings   between cream billows   hint of lace   folds   underneath   Is this life

a preparation   for a future one   little sparrow   perched   on a limb

外国人一人　　　　　　捕虜　　　　　　　　　串をケーキに変えた　　　　　　　日本

島　　　このバームクーヘンならず　　浮かぶ　　　　　　　ショートケーキの雲　　子供時代

その層を歩く　　　　　　　　　　　宮曼荼羅　　　　　　　　　　　　三笠山の麓

月満ち　　　　　　　上　　　　　　　影紙の丘のくぼみ　　　　　五人の

化身より高く　　　　　　森の情景を見守る　　　　地蔵菩薩も一人　　　空の母

地球の膣　　　待つ　　　　　　川の交じり　　　　　誰も眠り　　　　鹿

以外　　　　　　鳥居の外で跳ね合う　　　　　道が　　　　　　橋に導く

霧に消え　　　　　すやり霞垣間見　　　　葉なき枝　　　　半透明な幹

幽霊盛り土　　　　銀白の　　　　花　　　桃　　微かな地衣類緑の　　夢

静かな　　　曲がる小川　　　道はまた現れ　　　途切れる　　　寺　　傾く

広場　　　鳥瞰図　　　東方に向かい　　　記憶の　　聖なる間　　虚しい

輪　　　クリームの大波の間に　　　レースの影　　　襞の　　下　この命は

将来のものの　　　　　準備か　　　小さな雀　　　枝に　　　とまった

[*Sparrow.* 10 x 10 inches. Nepali highland green tea on paper.]

Who are you   outside the window?   You are   larger than my house

alert   open-eyed   I feed you grains   pet you   talk to you

You   return to my hand   flutter here   then there   so wild so free   You

sing your shō-flute melody   from the eaves   or the Himalayas   deep

in the Kasuga Forest   or a bamboo grove   You sip   the dews at Adashino

eat the seeds   from the moon's katsura tree   My life   wanes in its gaze

I fall ill and you visit me   hospital days   pass like waves   wash over

a sea pine   Leaves infuse   the leaves   with highland green   shades

passerine   Why   did you leave   in the middle of spring?

Once now once forever   Asuka River song   flowing   pools

yesterday   shallows   today   through the frames   of the ancestors

お前は誰　　　　　　　窓の外　　　　　　お前は　　　　　　私の家より大きい

機敏に　　　　目を開き　　　　私はお前に穀物を食べさせ　　　　撫で　　　話す

お前は　　　手に戻り　ここに飛び　それからあそこに　　　野生で自由　お前は

笙の奏を歌い　　　　　軒から　　　　　　またヒマラヤ　　　　　深く

春日の森に　　　　また竹藪　　　　　　お前は啜る　　　　化野の露

種子を食べ　　　　月の桂の木から　　　　私の命は　　　その凝視に劣ろい

病気になりお前は見舞う　　　　病院の日々　　　波のように通る　　海松を

洗う　　　　葉は　　　　葉に注ぐ　　　　高地緑の　　　　　陰

スズメ目　　　　　　何故　　　　　去ったのか　　　　　春の真中に

一度居れば永久に　　　　飛鳥川の歌　　　　　流れ　　　　溜まる

昨日　　　　浅い　今日　　　　祖先の　　　　　枠を通して

[*Ancestors*. 10 x 10 inches. Houji tea on paper.]

My everyday   childhood   comes back to me   in the images

at the entryway   the four   nō faces   staring down from the place

of honor   like immortals   tilting forward   toward   earth

Their presence   immutable   silence   ancestors   obscured by the

leaves   of the phantom tree   fading   from within   into

oblivion   a flash   reflected in glass   without   ceremony

Notes of a shakuhachi   intertwine with the limbs   A faint line

breaks   unevenly   divides the surface   into three: above   below

and elsewhere   Omamori   tassels   suspended two

by two   cushions   cross the plane's   absence   Life

once broken off   reappears again   diverse manifestations   Your cry

woke me up   from my reverie   tongue-cut sparrow

私の日々　　　　　子供時代　　　　　が蘇る　　　　　面影

入り口　　　　　四枚の　　　　　能面　　　　　上座から

凝視する　　　　仙人のよう　　　　前方に傾き　　　地面の　　　方に

それらの存在は　　　　不変の　　　沈黙　　　祖先　　　葉に

不透明　　　　幻の木　　　　薄れ　　　　中から　　　忘却

に　　　　閃き　　　　ガラスに映られ　　　　儀式　　　貼らず

尺八の音　　　　　肢体に絡む　　　　　微かな線が

折れ　　　不均等に　　　表面を分け　　　三つに　　上　　下

その他　　　　お守りの　　　　房　　　　二つ

ずつ　　　座布団　　　平面を渡る　　　不在　　　命は

一度折れ　　　また現れる　　　色々の形　　　お前の鳴き声が

初めて　　　　私を目覚め　　　　夢想から　　　舌切り雀

[*Tongue-cut sparrow.* 10 x 10 inches. Nepali highland green tea on paper.]

Empty bowl   once full of starch   you mistook for food   put out for you

tongue-cut sparrow   the little girl misses you   She grew

a new tongue too   far away from you   She cannot find   the words

She speaks   through the leaves   Kami spirit of the grove   green garment

bends with the wind's accord   What gives the heart   form?   A box

of treasures   or a box of monsters   whichever it deserves   Or

the box tamatebako   which will protect you from harm   if unopened

Otohime's parting gift to her   when she needed to go home   tend to her

elderly mother   She had stayed three days at the dragon palace on the ocean floor

the turtle she had saved brought her back   to the shore of her village   everything

unfamiliar   her house   gone   mother   gone   family

and friends   nowhere to be found   Only the myth of her name

passed between the lips of the strangers   the one who had vanished at sea three

hundred years ago   never to return   All alone   her despair   as she opened

the box   the white cloud of her old age   rushed out   hurried

into her body   Mortality   the heart's   single   autumn chrysanthemum

空の鉢　　　　　　かつて糊で一杯　　　　　自分に出してくれた　　　　食べ物と思った

舌切り雀　　　　　　小さな女の子はお前が恋しい　　　　　その子も

新しい舌が生えた　　　　　　君から遠く　　　　言葉が　　見つからない

葉の間から　　　　話す　　　藪神　　　　　緑衣は

風のままに曲がる　　　　何が心に形を　　　　与えるのか　　　宝物の

葛籠か　　　　怪物の葛籠か　　　　値する方　　　あるいは

玉手箱　　　　危害から守ってくれる　　　　開かなければ

乙姫のお別れの土産　　　　うちに戻るのに必要だった　　　年老いた母

の世話のため　　　　　　　女は海底の龍宮に三日泊まった

救っていた亀が連れ戻ってくれた　　　　村の海辺に　　　全て

見慣れぬ　　　家は　　　無く　　　母は　　　無く　　家族も

友達も　　　どこにもいない　　　　ただ彼女の名の神話だけが

人々の口に上った　　　　三百年前　　　海に消えた人

戻らなかった人　　　たった一人で　　　彼女の絶望　　　箱を

開く　　　その老齢の白雲が　　　走り出て　　　女の体に

急ぎ入る　　　寿命　　　心の　　一つの　　秋の菊

[*Kiku*. 10 x 10 inches. Sabbathday Lake Shaker chamomile tea on paper.]

Ikeru   place a flower in a vase to revive it   Ikeru   place a dead body in the earth

to bury it   A word   exists   to measure the world

however small   or immense   its affinities   Follows another   under-

current   Crystal-bead bubbles   surge into billows   kiku crest afloat

on the kettle   Out of the ash heap   a broken sprig   raised

from the mind's   refinery   immaculate memory   breathes out   earth

breathes in   heaven   scent of honey   Chrysanthemum   detached

garden blossom   as the leaves fall   blooms alone   before the bamboo border

pine   reflected in moonlight   water   Stem-cut petals overlap   into a ball

curl toward the crown's navel   hides a face   behind tongues of chamomile

flames   It tells me to   let go   no   home   left   to go   home

to   without her   Child   were you really   once the flower   who held the mirror?

活ける　　　　花を花瓶に入れ蘇らせる　　　　　　活ける　　　　死体を土に置き

埋める　　　　　言葉が一つ　　　　　　在り　　　　　　世界を測る

いかに小さく　　　　巨大であれ　　　　その類似性　　　従う別の　　　　地下

水　　　　水晶玉の泡が　　　　大波に急騰する　　　　　菊の紋浮かぶ

薬缶の上　　　　　灰の盛り上がりから　　　　折れた小枝　　　　頭の

精錬所　　　　曇りなき記憶から　　　　引き上げられ　　　土を　　　吐き出し

天を　　　　吸い込む　　　蜜の香り　　　　　菊　　　　離れた

庭の花　　　　葉が落ち　　　　　花だけ　　　　竹の境の前

松　　　　月光に映える　　　　水　　　茎で切った花弁が重なり　　　玉になり

王冠の臍に曲がる　　　　　　　顔を隠す　　　　　雛菊炎の舌の

後ろに　　　　私に言う　　　放せ　　家は　　　無い　　帰るべき　　　家は

彼女なしに　　　子供よ　　　かつてお前は本当に　　　鏡を持った　　　花だったのか

[*Sink*. 10 x 10 inches. Orange pekoe tea on paper.]

As if in a dream the cloud   filled the room   walls a wash of orange

pekoe   white down softness   the same syllables for paper   hair   deity

At the end of the hallway   it emerged   a sinkful of mist   up

against the frosted   glass lattice   angled in the oval mirror   ornately forged

Echo clear   glance of a raised sail   through a square porthole

broken   haze   Two small apothecary jars   pressed into a corner

backs to the edge   of a mosaic grid   Such infinite patience   objects

possess   dust   collects   time's passing indifference   glows

on the other side   of the window   the lizards cling to   after the rain

passes through   Can you remember   each day at the well?

Washing your hands   and face   its devotion   to your

cleanliness   keeping yesterday   the same as today   now

looking back   at the smile   of Mother's   presence

まるで夢のように雲が　　　　　　　　部屋を満たし　　　　　　　壁はオレンジ

ペコーの一塗り　　　　　白羽毛の柔らかさ　　　　　紙　　　　髪　　　　神と同じ音

廊下の端に　　　　　　現れた　　　　　　流し台一杯の霧が上がる　　　　　ぼんやりした

ガラス格子のこちら側　　　　　卵形鏡を斜交いに　　　　　華美な鋳造　　　　響明らかな

上がった帆の一瞥　　　　　四角の船窓を通し　　　　　　　破れた　　　　　　　霞

二つ小さな薬剤師の壺　　　　　　　角に押し込まれ　　　　　背は　　モザイク格子

の端　　　　　　　そんな無限の根気　　　　　　　　　物は取り付き

埃は　　　　　　集まる　　　　　　　　　　　　時の過ぎる無関心は

光る　　　　　　雨が通ったあと　　　　　　　　　　　　　　蜥蜴たち

の吸い付く　　　　　　　　窓の向こう側に　　　　　　　思い出せるか

井戸の其々の日を　　　　　手と　　　　　　　　　顔を洗いながら

君の清潔さへの　　　　　献身　　　　　　昨日を保つ　　　今日と同じく

今　　　　　見返す　　　　　母の姿の　　　　　　　微笑みを

[*Mother.* 10 x 10 inches. Houji tea on paper.]

Silence mother of sound   arriving   receding   Form   nō other

than emptiness   emptiness   nō other than form   accommodates

everything   She is happy to see me   her eighty-year-old spirit   with secrets

to share with me   Changeless flower   her happiness   as deep as the mountains

shaded wrinkles   of houjicha   her favorite leaves   steeped   stems

stacked sweetness   traced to the slope's soil   roasted grain   Sun   mist

sip Issa   cup of water   and heat   She gave me   a life   with love   raised

me my happiness   hers   grew with me   She was there   at the Jiba

the coming-home place   of glass   paper   wood   stone   One day

she   let me go   and I crossed the sea   for another island   the flame

within me   burned intently   more intensely   transformed   Her

likeness   her bright   child-gaze   her face   brushed onto the page

will it be washed away   by the light?   Mother   how vast

is this grove   without you   where is my home   where is

not   my home   empty   nō-bird   nest

沈黙は音の母　　　　　　到着し　　　　後退する　　　　色　　　　空以外の

能　　　　　　　　空　　　　　　　　　色以外の能　　　　　　　全てを

受け入れる　　　　　　私に会うのが嬉しい　　　　傘寿の意気　　　　　分かつ

秘密　　　　　　変化なき花　　　　　　幸せ　　　　　　　山ほど深く

陰影ある皺　　　　焙じ茶　　　　その好きな葉　　　　浸した　　　　茎

積まれた甘味　　　　坂の土に戻る　　　　焙じた穀物　　　太陽　　　霧

一茶を啜る　　　一杯の水　　そして熱　　　私に　　　愛を以って　　命をくれた

私を私の幸せを育て　　　彼女の幸せも　　　私と育った　　そこに居た　　　地場

帰郷の場　　　　ガラス　　　　紙　　　　木　　　　石の　　　或る日

彼女は　　　　放した　　　　そして私は海を渡って　　　別の地に　　炎は

私の内に　　　強く燃えた　　　もっと強く　　　変貌した　　　その人の

類似　　　明るい　　子供の眼差し　　　　その顔　　　　頁に書き込まれ

洗いされるだろうか　　　光で　　　母親　　　　いかに巨大なのか

薮　　　お前無しに　　　　　私の家はどこに　　　　どこに

私の家はないのか　　　　　　空　　　　　　能鳥　　　　巣

IV

"It's early, or it's late"

It's early, or it's late,
in the darkness

You knock
but the door wouldn't open

      your typed drafts in an open box
      on the light wood floor

      your open spines stretched
      along the half-wall shelves

      at the table
      where we once sat
      talking

      tea poured
      into the room
            like sunlight
      in the afternoon

      laughter
      the days to come

            Behind you
      on the wall

      "called back"
      rubbed from the stone

to some autotelic *island*
of no going beyond

here

to understand more than to know
you said with silence

listening

for the words
for
your arrival

for Jean Valentine (1934–2020)

Sea Birth   See Day

Set out on East Slope   to tend the abandoned fort
plow   anchored to dirt   plot cleared
of overgrowth   tilled words   spaces
for silence   carved seal   sown   seed-
bed   to field   even   lines   of seedling
stands   breath watering greenery   trans-
planted   signs   through your warmth   of mind
generosity of time   what you taught
of the fire   bearing words to the light
guided by fire   the source: fire   *struck by Apollo*
caught   dazed   afloat in the half-light   Helios
arc   your periplum   drawing the stars to our shore-
lines   your work *Schatzkarte*   or *carte aux trésors*
coordinates   Provençal geography with *Gironde*'s
rough sheafs   shadows Walter and Asja on a sleigh
through the bitter cold of Moscow's streets   *Animosity
and love . . . shifting within me like winds*   your sustaining
ear   sage   depths' fuse and spark   translates
dichten   as *condensare*   anima into aura   meta-
morphic bridge   across   abysm   sea   birth
see day   time's inflorescence   threshed grains
distilled   *historical aftereffects*   in intro   chronology
afterword   your grinding Lenz   suffers
the madness of boredom   bordering   nonexistence
you who   smuggle salt onto our tongues   your
poetry   sings both hymns and fragments   *drunk
with light*   *and the spirit of animals*   *rests with them*
you   instigator at the cliff's edge   of the over-
looked romance   the forgotten key   scaled

to the whole relation   margin   merges to center

reverse   sunfish decomposition   *to material*

of extraordinary magnitude   periplum bathed

in the glow of the footlights   friendly

echo of Sylvie   twice lost   facing the *cité*

merveilleuse   (*et* Aurélia   appears in the vision's

mirror)   your prophecies   your geometries   your

love and emblems of Délie   being   moon & sun

your unreal cities   chimeras   dreams   Labé

dying of that Love   Which slays me ten thousand times

a day   your chrysalis and Plume   days quiet

making a sign   peak, abyss on the same line   rest

at the interval   remission's gift: for us

enriched   belonging here   in our *late*

civilization   Richard   heart's accord   embarked

upon   the circle's seventh arc   shaded

by the leaves of Tyrol   in Ratzes   by the Schlern

towering dolomite peaks   talus reef   attuned

to   the *hurlahei of the stream*   the nightingale

the thrush   the morels   and bellflowers

straw stalks   wind   a ruin of walls dissipating fog

and the wolves   howling   at the lion's feet

for Richard Sieburth

Coral for Kamau

We grow upon our dead
and flourish   the pain
that *swims into the polyp's eye*
my yellow pain   grain   of sand
sea's memory   sees the limestone garden
ten thousand eyes   hidden   beneath the surface
of the mirror-
blue water   I and I   dive   through the liquid
syllables   to the bones of the island   hear
the flowering
ocean's tongue   *the amorous answering chorus of sound*
living
reef dub   in *son*   in *adowa*   in *calypso*   lim-
bo   sum of sun   indwelling force
of spirit
between body   and soul
in *nam*
colony   breeds colony   contingent chirality
temperate needs
of each body   inside another
body   sunlight depths
tidal
patience   plastid
moons
illuminate   the endosymbiont genome   clades
within clades   methylating
silence   light and dark   reactions
photosynthate   energy   transfer
budding clusters of   dreaming
planula
drift   and drift and   settle
home   choral   happiness
you've   left us   now   no-death
loa   at the crossroads   Legba   *thunder-*
stone   Negus   it is   it is

135

```
              not                    dawn
after dawn              after
      words      bloom           with us        in
         us           for            I              and I
           to untie                    the nets
                     from the belly
                         of the whale
```

in memory of Kamau Brathwaite (1930–2020)

V

Ancestors

Chance progression

Genomic drift

Split-apart generations
of the uprooted tree

abandoned the tablets for another ethos

Ancestors

never spoke of our ancestors

watching over through
the great- great- void

behind the incense and flowers

brought us here

     In this quiet room
to learn from the old and make the new

Hakgojae 學古齋

Gallery, east of the Joseon
Palace of Shining Happiness

       young and old stroll in hanbok cosplay
       under full autumn sun

       coco capitán mirrors herself outside west gate

       fi lee inks the stillness rite on a Buamdong hill

siren eun young jung channels the yeo-
song gukgeuk with anomalous fantasies

her reinventions of the forgotten 1950s women's theater, lost
memories performed through dance and song, her impulse

Hakgojae

a practice of living art
as a dream of a living

presence

      Drawn into the wood

              across the sea of stone

      one approaches
as if to recognize
the unexpected

spark and hesitation
underground

double-track spotlights
on the five wood figures, octagon universe

They look out from the ghostly grain
of the tall tablet doorway, two-
and-a-half vertical planks, dark altar portrait
painted on wood, mounted pieces of wood
shades move in seasons, eyes in the tree

the eldest sits in a chair, painted white, cut-out
      raised body, hanbok strips, mountainous roots
      dress floats past the doorway plane,
      head straight, her half-smiling face

the youngest sits cross-legged on the ground, brown dress,
      head tilts right, hair in a bun, gentle face anther ear,
      half-moon smile, her body curves beyond
      the door, strong hands cuddle a fuzzy white dog
above her in dusty red, she sits higher
      than the eldest, head tilts left, folded
      hands unpainted knot, side curls of hair,
      eyes bright lotus petals, line nose to brow
at the center the second eldest stands tallest, cut-out head
      straight to collar, blouse white, a quarter of her face
      sliced clean against rings, her lower body unpainted
      wood wrinkles, waves, mouth small serious face
next to her in fading forest green she stands shorter
      behind the eldest, body cropped at the left
      shoulder down the door's edge, head tilts right
      cut-out wood piece to chest, oval face wavy hair

No figure whole, the youngest closest to wholeness

simplest gestures of line and ink, faces
manifest the inner essence
of the salvaged wood, pith to heart-
wood, sapwood dies to heartwood, spiral
mysteries, half-deities

      And behind them
            the falls
      of a teal blue curtain
      heaven-scent drifts
            red
      earth pools on the floor
      in front of them, low
      wood hills, flat clouds
           a rock, a flame

After the two hanji portraits framed on the walls
at the room's entrance—preparatory or ancillary

to the wood incarnation—the same women posed
with variations, one interior: yellow umber backdrop,
          brown ground, light yellow three-plank tablet tree
          rings swirl up twice as high behind them—
the other exterior: on a lotus field, they float
          on huge lotus leaves, self-cleansing lotus
          stems strong bud to flower, grow from mud
          into purity, summer family *dreaming*
          in a situation of oppression

          Vibrant minhwa colors of the people, pictures
anonymous artisans made for everyday dream
and longevity, happiness and harmony, springing out
from the literati and court tradition into ch'aekkori
"look at the shelves of books, paper, brushes,"
hwajodo flowers and birds, hodo tigers (smiling),
yongdo dragon on the front gate, kirin and dog, fish
and crab, rooster on the inner gate illuminates
the night, totemic decoy guards and protects

minhwa blessings
for the miraculous order of the universe

Ancestors

follow ancestors
through the changes

          nature's renewal
source and being

hidden energies
exist

through her *We are*
a matrilineal family

Yun Suknam

      transformed
into the image
of the vision in the wood

                      for Kim Hyesoon and Yun Suknam

Acknowledgments

"Langkasuka" was written after a stay in Kuala Lumpur in 2012, as a guest of Eddin Khoo, Pauline Fan, and their cultural organization Pusaka (pusaka.org). All thanks to them for its inception and existence. Sources for the poems include *Spirit of Wood: The Art of Malay Woodcarving* by Farish A. Noor and Eddin Khoo (Periplus Editions, 2003); *Taming the Winds of Desire: Psychology, Medicine, and Aesthetics in Malay Shamanistic Performance* (University of California Press, 1991) and *Wives and Midwives: Childbirth and Nutrition in Rural Malaysia* (University of California Press, 1983/1987) by Carol Laderman; *Tao Te Ching: A Bilingual Edition*, translated by D. C. Lau (The Chinese University of Hong Kong Press, 2001); *The Shadow Puppet Theatre of Malaysia* by Beth Osnes (McFarland & Company, Inc, 2010), *Malay Magic* by Walter W. Skeat (Oxford University Press, 1984), *An Analysis of Malay Magic* by K. M. Endicott (Oxford University Press, 1970), *Kelantan: Religion, Society and Politics in a Malay State* edited by William R. Roff (Oxford University Press, 1974), *Magic and Divination in Malay Illustrated Manuscripts* by Farouk Yahya (Brill, 2016), *Le Théatre d'ombres à Kelantan* by Jeanne Cuisinier (Gallimard, 1957), *Folk Literature of the Selknam Indians: Martin Gusinde's Collection of Selknam Narratives* edited by Johannes Wilbert (UCLA Latin American Center Publications, 1975), and *A Record of the Buddhist Religion in India and the Malay Archipelago: AD 671–695* by I-Tsing, translated by J. Takakusu (Clarendon Press, 1896; Munshiram Manoharlal, 1966, 1982).

Some of the poems first appeared in *Almost Island: The Past* (Winter 2020)—thanks to Sharmistha Mohanty, Souradeep Roy, and Rahul Soni; *The Georgia Review* (Fall 2021)—thanks to Gerald Maa; *FE* (Fonograf Editions, 2022)—thanks to Jeff Alessandrelli, Adie Bovee, and John Goodhue; *Granta* (online, Spring 2022)—thanks to Rachael Allen; *Poetics for the More-Than-Human World*, edited by Mary Newell, Bernard Quetchenbach, and Sarah Nolan (Dispatches Editions, 2020)—thanks to the editors; and *Rhinozeros. Europa im Übergang*, edited by Priya Basil, Franck Hofmann, Teresa Koloma Beck, and Markus Messling (Volume 1: *Reparien*; Matthes & Seitz, 2020)—thanks to Priya Basil and Beatrice Fassbinder.

Eternal gratitude to Eddin Khoo and Mahesan Selladurai for the photographs of the *wayang kulit*. The two pohon beringin images © Mahesan Selladurai. *Purnama* © Eddin Khoo.

"Line and Light" was written for Melissa McGill's *Constellation*, a sculptural project installed in the ruins of Bannerman's Castle on Pollepel Island in the Hudson River from June 2015 to October 2017, and published in her book *Constellation* (Princeton Architectural Press, 2015). It first appeared in the Spring 2015 issue of *BOMB*—thanks to Mónica de la Torre and Betsy Sussler.

Eternal gratitude to Melissa McGill for the night and day photographs of *Constellation*, both © Melissa McGill.

"Ceiling and Time" was written for the centennial celebration of Grand Central Terminal organized by MTA Arts & Design and the Poetry Society of America in 2013—thanks to Alice Quinn for the invitation that sparked the occasion. It first appeared in *A Public Space: No. 21*—thanks to Brett Fletcher Lauer and Brigid Hughes. Here it has been substantially revised.

A fragment of what would become "Stones and Stars" was written for Brandon Shimoda's blog post at *futurefeed*, "The Afterlife, Part 4: The Ancestors Reside in the Answers Themselves." A slightly different version of the final poem first appeared in *Together in a Sudden Strangeness*, edited by Alice Quinn (Knopf, 2020).

Thanks to Randall Martin Design for the technical help in the scanning and conversion of Kazumi Tanaka's drawings in "No Home Go Home / Go Home No Home." And to Hiroaki Sato for blessing the poem with his translations. Thanks also to Margaret Mitsutani for her helpful feedback on the translations. A different version of the "Note" was posted on the *Daily*, the blog of the *Paris Review*, where six of the poems and images first appeared in the Summer 2017 issue—thanks to Robyn Creswell and Lorin Stein. A limited fine-art letterpress edition of the project will be published by Arion Press in San Francisco—thanks to Rolph Blythe, Susie Bright, and Blake Riley.

"Sea Birth   See Day" was written for Richard Sieburth on occasion of his seventieth birthday and the celebratory edition *En Face & Beieinander: Festschrift for Richard Sieburth*, edited by Sage Anderson, Paul Fleming, John Hamilton, and Daniel Hoffmann-Schwartz (N.p., 2019), and subsequently revised. The earlier draft first appeared in the Winter 2018 issue of *Almost Island*—thanks to Vivek Narayanana and the other editors noted above.

"Coral for Kamau" first appeared in *Lana Turner: No. 13*—thanks to Cal Bedient and David Lau.

"Ancestors" was written after a visit to Seoul with Don Mee Choi and Christopher Mattison as guests of LTI Korea in 2019. It first appeared in the Winter 2019 issue of the *Paris Review*—thanks to Vijay Seshadri, Lauren Kane, and Emily Nemens. Thanks also to the Hakgojae Gallery and Yun Suknam for permission to use the photograph of *We are a matrilineal family*, 2018. Image © Yun Suknam. Courtesy of Hakgojae Gallery, Seoul.

Thanks, always, to Jeff Shotts—*il miglior editor*—Fiona McCrae, Katie Dublinski, Marisa Atkinson, Casey O'Neil, Chantz Erolin, and the rest of the Graywolf Press staff.

And to Silvia Fehrmann, Laura Muñoz-Alonso, and the DAAD Berliner Künstlerprogramm.

A last shout out to Michelle, Arjun, and Qingxi; to my mother and sister and family; to friends, young and old; and to Marble and Bergamot—*both rabbits, sidebyside, earth running* ("Mu Lan's Song," tr. Eric Sackheim).

Jeffrey Yang is the author of the poetry collections *Hey, Marfa,* winner of the Southwest Book Award and chosen as a Best Book of the Year by the *New York Times* and *Library Journal; Vanishing-Line;* and *An Aquarium,* winner of the PEN/Joyce Osterweil Award. He is the editor-at-large at New Directions Publishing.

The text of *Line and Light* is set in Arno Pro.
Book design by Rachel Holscher.
Composition by Bookmobile Design and Digital
Publisher Services, Minneapolis, Minnesota.
Manufactured by Friesens on acid-free,
100 percent postconsumer wastepaper.